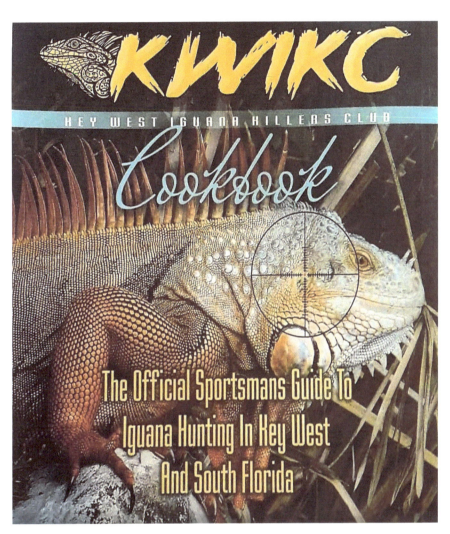

By Charles Meier

Photo Credits
Charles Meier, Taya Anzano, Angel Diaz, Dylan Slaunwhite, Casey Collins, Josh Collins

Edited by:
Laura A. Mayesing

Written by
Charles Meier

If you are not reading a color version one is available on Creatspace.com, This book is also available on Kindle.

Cover Book Design
Jim Walton at Farm Snipers

Most of this information was taken from Wikipedia.com a free online encyclopedia, the Florida Department of Agriculture, and the Guinness Book of World Records.

COPYRIGHT 2017
ISBN:-13:978-1981899692
ISBN:-10:1981899693

All rights reserved, no part of this book may be reproduced without permission from the Publisher unless in review form.

Special Thanks

I would like to thank all the people of Key West who have helped to make this happen.

I would also like to thank some of the haters out there whom have attempted and at times succeeded in getting me banned from Social Media Platforms such as Face Book. I've realized that society has defaulted to some pansy ass world of Political correctness and Snowflake sensitivity. i.e. (Everyone is entitled to an opinion, as long as it's the same as ours.)

Apparently, in today's age that is the key to success. It would seem that the current rule is "if you don't agree with someone immediately throw a temper tantrum, scream, cry, call them names, and make violent threats to the offending party, attack them in all manor possible, then run to a safe place have your mommy pet your head, because in the real world none of that made the BAD MAN GO AWAY.

So, as you can tell even through all the past trials and tribulations during the great snowflake blizzard of 2017 It didn't stop me at all. As a matter of fact, it was the driving force that motivated me to continue just for spite. Uhh, I mean the opportunity to educate people about the island we live on and the actual iguana problem in South Florida and the Florida Keys, and yes even the different opinions of people regarding this problem. Of course, as you now know, I added a few solutions to the current invasive species issue.

I would also like to thank all the chef's, restaurants and old timers who provided some insight on different Iguana recipes. Jose' and his wife down at Jose's II, located in Key West. Whom have graciously hosted several wild iguana dinners or as Americans put it, exotic game dinners using old world Nicaraguan recipes, and Jose' & Tommy at Blossoms Cajun Kitchen in Key West for providing a little Cajun flair and some new cooking and dining experiences.

I'll keep on killing and chilling, if you guys keep on grilling.

This book dedicated first and foremost to my family, especially my wife and daughter

Dallis & Taya.

For putting up with

me and all my wild ideas.

Oh yeah and a special thanks to my wife Dallis for getting me started in iguana sniping.

My hunting partners:

Taya, Angel, & Dylan

For providing tactical support and more permanent solutions to the lizard problem in the ongoing iguana war.

Next, to my friends both new and old whom are just getting into or have been Iguana hunting for a while now. And the rest of you all that hang around to buy my books or just to see what kind of crap I'm going to stir up next.

Love you guys and thanks for the support.

Contents

Welcome to the Iguana killers club.
About the Author.
Warning This is not a safe zone.
What's the Goal?
Iguana's. So, what's the problem.
How did they get here?
Learning before you buy.
Don't let it lose.
The Gene is out of the bottle.
How did I get into this?
The birth of the I.K.C.
How can you get into this?
Love the haters.
Remember only you can prevent an iguana invasion.
How do you find iguanas to hunt?
Tools of the trade.
Rules of Gun Safety.
Shot placement.
No carcass, no credit.
Using pets to patrol the area.
Know your foe. Part of the iguana and Iguana danger signs.
The dewlap.
Head bobbing.
Tongue flicking.
Posturing.
Squirming.

Charging.
Tail whipping.
The bite.
The total package in the predatory concept.
How to eat an iguana.
Gross, Disgusting, eat a lizard (What's in a name)
Baby steps.
Field dressing you lizard.
What does iguana taste like?
My first experience.

Recipes

Boiled Iguana eggs.
BBQ Iguana.
Iguana Soup.
Iguana Stew.
Iguana Pinole.
Sweet Teriyaki iguana.
Cajun style Iguana legs or Dragons wings.
Key West Mojo marinated iguana.
Iguana Taco.
Trinidad Style Curry iguana stew.

Drinks

World famous Green iguana margarita.
Sleeping lizard.
Iguana sunrise.
Naked iguana.
Pink iguana.

Closing.

Other books by Charles BIGDADDY Meier

Special Thanks.

The Iguana Killers Club

Welcome to the Key West island backyard safari:

killing, chilling, and grilling. Dock to dish, porch to plate, grab a fork, and don't be late. From the top of the tree to the frying pan, don't forget the beans and rice, my man. Grab a cold beer and a couple of limes, the iguana will be done just in time.

About the Author

My name is Charles Meier; I'm originally from a small town called Fredericksburg, Texas. I've been a resident of the Florida Keys since the U.S. Navy dropped me off here in 1992.

Since that time, I've done a lot of stuff: trials, tribulations, and of course several misadventures. I've been a rescue swimmer, firefighter, police officer, worked on the S.W.A.T & Dive Team for the Monroe County Sheriff's Department, a strip club manager, a DJ, a boat captain, a pirate, a Viking, a minister, a mercenary, and a motivational speaker. For the purposes of this book, I'm the island air gunner, the iguana assassin, the critter getter, or the island iguana sniper. I've been around the world twice and probably talked to everybody at least once, been shot at and missed, shit at and hit, blown up six times in my life, three of them being in the same day.

Hell, I've documented a few of my misadventures in the fine form of fancy reading material such as the publication you're perusing through now. I'll be the first to say I'm no Hemingway, but my rantings are always fun and informative. And yes, they sometimes even piss people off.

I've attempted to escape this island several times, but something just keeps dragging me back to it. I'm not sure if it's the sun, the sand, the senoritas, the margaritas or if it's the laid-back toes in the water, ass in the sand island lifestyle that sucks me back like a tractor beam. Whatever the cause, I've made this rock, which is strategically placed between the Gulf of Mexico, and the Atlantic Ocean, and 90 miles from the coast of Cuba my home; I'm not leaving anytime soon.

Remember when I said this book may piss people off?

If you are a herpetologist, have a pet lizard, or live in some place that has a cold winter that will kill every iguana you see, you may not understand this book. If you are a vegan, if you are not a hunter, or you are all touchy feely and love all animals big and small, or you just like iguanas, you defiantly will not understand this book.

The Florida Keys unfortunately, is currently under attack from an all-out iguana invasion. There are only two sides of the fence to stand on.

I like iguana's and don't want anyone to kill them because they're not doing anything, there cute, they were here first, and you sir are (insert expletive here). And some would even go as far as including some death threats in their rants. These actions usually come from keyboard commandos, locked in safety of their basements in lands far, far away.

Or

Iguanas are destroying everything on the island and we need to do something about it! They suck. They're ugly, they shit on everything, they have eaten all my plants, and that big orange one over there just tried humping my neighbor's cat. Well, it would seem that I'm that guy. The one with the most permanent solutions to the current iguana problems.

This book describes small game hunting, shot placement, catching, killing, cleaning and cooking iguanas. Several different recipes that you can make with iguana as the main ingredient. And beverages that of course will help you wash down your exotic game dinner. If you're not into that I'll give you option number two: We're defending a very fragile Florida eco system from non-indigenous invasive species, that is rapidly overrunning the island and South Florida and saving butterflies, burrowing land turtles, owls and trees.

You see, a little something for everybody.

The iguana problem is location specific. If you're from anywhere in what we (on the island) call the north which of course also depends on your geographical location in the Keys. For instance, someone from Key West believes that ten miles up the road is north. If you're in Marathon, Florida you would believe Key Largo and Miami is north. Everyone in the Florida Keys considers any place that must deal with frost in the morning north.

That of course includes those frozen tundra's like California, Colorado, Utah, Minnesota, Michigan, and yes even Jacksonville, Florida.

If you are from any of the aforementioned locations on the planet you may not truly understand this book and how bad the iguana invasion has become.

What's the Goal?

Education, telling people about the current iguana problem which if not controlled now will lead to an iguana epidemic in South Florida and giving people the means to attempt to be a part of the solution.

 Now with that being said, if you are from South Florida or more importantly the fabulous Florida Keys this is an invitation to step outside of your comfort zone and go on a back-yard island safari with me.

Iguanas

So, what's the problem?

If you are not from Key West, or South Florida that's a very good question, I'm so glad that you asked. In the last five to ten years South Florida and now the Florida Keys have been overrun by iguanas. It's ground zero for the iguana invasion. So as one may be able to tell, I find it mildly amusing that some people will still ask, "What's an iguana?"

The simple answer is a big ass lizard. This is where I go all geek on you and drop a little background info. If you consult the fine people of Wikipedia you will get the text book definition of iguana. Stating that, "...iguana is derived from the Spanish form of the Taino name for this animal is actually, iwana."

Who were the Tanio's?

Another great question, the Tanio's were the original inhabitants of the Antilles and the Bahaman Islands.

The iguana was first officially described as a species by Swedish botanist Carolus Linnaeus in 1758. It's native to tropical areas of Central and South America and the Caribbean.

There are approximately 17 different species of iguana but the ones we are concerned with are the Black Iguana a.k.a. The Spiney's or *Ctenosaura Similes*. It was originally native to Mexico and Central America but was somehow introduced to South Florida. Most experts believe it was the pet trade.

This is one of the largest species of the genus *Ctenosaura*; the males can get up to 50 inches or four feet in length and the females just a little smaller. And they have some speed to them.

The fine people at the Guinness Book of World Records say that this little leather encased spiked backed speed demon can hit speeds of 21.7mph. That sir, is the fastest lizard on the planet.

As of this writing the Spinney's seem to be located in one area on Big Pine Key. Centrally located near an old coral quarry. Of course, all of this is subject to change without the express written permission of anyone at any time. Natural selection, evolution, and lack of concern until it's too late.

The one that I and several of my friends at the Department of Agriculture believe are currently more prevalent in the Florida Keys is the Green Iguana.

The Green Iguana was more commonly found in pet stores but that is no longer the case.

If you venture a drive anywhere in South Florida or the Florida Keys, you will see them all over.

All you have to do is look anywhere: on the road sides, canals, parks, mangroves, palm trees, and even the cemetery.

It's more like a tour of Jurassic Park than a drive down US-1 to the islands. Florida has become so over populated with iguanas that in the winter time if we get a nice cold snap it literally starts raining iguanas.

Because they are a reptiles, they can't regulate their body temperature and just start falling out of the trees.

If you have never seen a large adult iguana fall out of a tree and smash into your vehicle, structure, or conveyance you are in for a rude awakening.

Nothing says bad day like getting knocked out by a 10,15, or even 20-pound iguana falling out of a palm tree.

It's not unusual to see big males reaching two meters (six-foot-long), and weighing in as much as 20 pounds.

This is not the cute little pet you bought for your kid, we're talking miniature dinosaurs here folks.

These animals have adapted to the area. They are smart, resilient, and have as many lives as a black cat. They have no natural predators and the ability to breed like rats.

It is estimated that the average Green Iguana has the ability to lay anywhere from 40 - 70 eggs in a clutch. The eggs hatch any time between 70 - 90 days depending upon location of the den, temperature, humidity, and other geographical conditions.

Iguanas are considered a non-indigenous invasive species by Florida Department of Agriculture. Which means they are enemy #1!

There is no season, size or bag limit. In laymen terms, it's open season 24/7/365.

You can kill as many as you want wherever you want (as long as you are on private property, or you have permission to hunt on the property, and you are killing them humanely).

On the East Coast of the United States, their range is from the Florida Keys all the way up the Broward counties. On the Gulf Coast side from the Florida Keys to Pinellas County and the Tampa Bay area.

How did they get here?

The general consensuses are the most common natural ways iguanas have arrived in the Keys could possibly be as stowaways on ships that carried fruits from South America, or rafting on vegetation that were blown into the Florida Keys from hurricanes and storms. However, the most likely cause is, of course, man. Pet owners who have bought them when they were cute little green lizards then one day they outgrew their cage, environment, and cuteness. Maybe they reached a breeding cycle and got a little testy or maybe even bit one of the family members. It would be at that point the owner didn't want to take care of them anymore. They became too much of a hassle to deal with, at which point, they were conveniently either released or escaped into the wild.

The Department of Agriculture has estimated that **Green Iguanas,** have resided in Florida since the 1960s, but their population has greatly increased since Hurricane Andrew in 1992. Although Green Iguanas have not had ecological impacts, this Central and South American lizard causes significant economic damage to landscape plants, primarily in Miami-Dade and Broward counties. On Florida's west coast, **black spiny tail iguanas** have reached such abundance that many residents view them as a nuisance, and the town of Boca Grande has hired trappers to remove them. There is a fellow by the name of George Cera. This man is the original iguana assassin and is accredited with killing over 16,000 iguanas in Boca Grande, Florida alone. And that was in 2009. Another friend of mine (Jim Walten) who runs a pest removal business called Farm Snipers. He frequently goes to Puerto Rico to hunt invasive iguanas, and has told me that there are approximately 4 million people and 8 million iguanas. On his trips he and his team of shooters rack out about 1,600 lbs. of iguana in a hunting session. "They are literally in every tree."

That is what is coming to Florida in the very near future if something is not done immediately.

It is estimated the iguana numbers are now into the millions and can live literally anywhere from creeks, waterways, farms, mangrove swamps, trees, and beaches. They have even adapted to more urban environments such as: drainage ditches, pipes, under houses, in attics, sheds, junkyards, boats, vehicles, and even cemeteries.

From personal experience there's nothing like walking through a graveyard and seeing a three or four-foot lizard slither into or out from under a grave stone or a grave that they have recently dug out a burrow under.

Somehow that has the ability to set the creep factor way up on the chart. Especially If you're in the cemetery right about the time the sun is setting, and you are a witness to this awesome event, it just adds bonus points.

Learn before you buy.

Before buying an exotic pet, or any pet you have to ask yourself a few questions:

- How big will this animal get?
- What does this animal eat?
- Am I prepared to care for this animal for 15-20 years?
- If not, who will?

Don't let it lose.

Letting an exotic animal lose after it has lost its luster is the main cause of the problem. If you can't care for an exotic pet anymore, don't set it free - that's illegal, and your pet will likely die without care from you. Some things you can do other than letting it go. Use the internet.

- Find a friend, family, local hobby group or rescue that may have an adoption program.
- See if the pet shop will take it back or accept it as a donation.
- Check your local nature centers and museums.
- Talk to your humane society.
- The Key West Sheriff's department has a petting zoo and takes donations of exotics such as these animals.
- Bring it to an **Exotic Pet Amnesty Day** or call the FWC's adoption hotline at 888-IVE-GOT1.

The genie is out of the bottle.

Nothing becomes a problem until it directly or indirectly causes you to receive pain or loss of money which of course goes back to pain!

I'm here to tell you that Iguana's do both. The monitory damage that iguanas have caused in South Florida is estimated to be in the millions. Not only are they a dangerous threat to Florida's fragile eco system. They are a very real threat to the general public.

Iguanas cause property damage by burrowing under houses, docks, decks, and sea walls to build tunnels dens and lay their eggs causing structural damage. They defecate on and in cars, boats, pool decks, sidewalks, pools, ponds, and anything with standing water.

Iguanas are known to carry salmonella and iguana eggs that are buried in a nest are considered to be HAZARDOUS WASTE due to that whole salmonella thing. That my friends, is just another little bonus.

They are a very real threat is to Florida's agricultural system. They eat every form of vegetation that is around: fruits, vegetables, garden plants, especially any form of flora, fauna that one may have planted as a yard beautification project. From the top of the flower, the leaves, and right down to the root.

In short, my professional opinion, iguanas are a plague of biblical proportion in the Florida Keys.

How did I get into this?

Well, it goes back to that pain and loss of money issue. In the past, I never had a problem with iguanas. As a matter of fact, up to a certain point in my life I thought they were kind of cool. And still to this day under certain circumstances they still are.

Here's the disclaimer: I'll tell you just like I have told my neighbors in the past, "If you take care of them properly and are a good pet owner, you and your iguana are not part of the problem."

Of course, look what we just did, we put people back into the equation and there in-lies the problem.

Most people don't make good pet owners. If you have a leash on your lizard, feed it, water and take care of it, you my friend are good to go.

If you got one from the store because little Suzy or little Jonny wanted one, and one day noticed that your lizard got big or bit your kid and you let it go because your give a damn was broken. YATZEEE! You are the culprit!

So here is the story of how I got into the lizard killing business.

One day a few years back my wife went down to the Home Depot; she bought a pickup truck load of plants for one of those previously mentioned home beautification projects.

She spent all day prepping, planning, preparing her garden, making sure that everything was exactly where it was supposed to be. When the sun went down she saw it was good, said it was good and by God it was good. So, flash forward to that the very next morning, she wanted to show me her beautiful accomplishment and advised that I should come out to the front porch and gaze upon the wonderment thereof.

I gathered myself up, grabbed a nice steaming cup of *café' conleche* and meandered out to the front porch to take a gander at the new home and garden beatification project. Upon my arrival I noticed my wife was speechless and in shock. She was just staring over a barren wasteland of what I assumed used to be a very beautifully planned out and orchestrated front yard flower garden, which now had been reduced to stems, a few twigs and a bunch of fine mulch. Of course, one of the perpetrators of this heinous crime was still in the garden munching on the very last bloom of a bougainvillea bush or something similar.

To say this woman was mad would be an understatement. She went from mad to plaid and back again. My wife went full Duke Nukem, did not pass go and initiated the scorched earth policy.

She had already tried all the other ways that they tell you to keep the green meanies away. Traps, sprays, pepper plants, burnt hair, you name it, she tried it and as you may have noticed, nothing worked. It was like a little green zombie invasion.

I believe it was at this time, shall we say, the line in the sand had been drawn and the kid gloves were yanked off.

My loving wife now has opted to use a more permanent solution. I believe it's called DEATH!

Now gentle reader, as you may know not much escapes death. The thought process is DEAD lizards don't eat flowers, foliage, little hatching baby birds or butterfly larva. And death has the unique ability to solve a lot of life's little vermin problems in the neighborhood.

Being an avid hunter, I was not going to let this opportunity pass me by without at least waiving at it.

So I may have mentioned, "You know baby, I really hate seeing you like this, and I want to do whatever it takes to make you happy..."

(as I fondly remembered the old adage, happy wife, happy life). Gentleman, I'm going to be using this opportunity for all its worth.

That being said, "...with the proper pellet rifle I could promote the finer principles of problem solving through the proper placement of propellant driven projectiles and reach out anywhere in the neighborhood with pin point precision and eradicate these little pesky vermin for you."

That's right, I was plotting iguana deaths from my perch on the front porch. Looking at the inner locking fields of fire, contemplating obstacles and objects that may get in my way. Organizing plans of attack. I had 30 to 80 yards of reach out and touch some leaping lizard action.

As they say, hell hath no fury like a woman scorned, and they my friends, are correct.

With that statement the purse strings of the war department were opened, and the coffers spilled out onto the floor.

My beautiful little wife who was still in the process of grieving over her freshly decimated flower garden gave me a blank check to retrieve the most lethal air rifle of my choice to unleash havoc upon my newly found foe. And that's how the Key West Chapter of the **Iguana Killers Club** (I.K.C) was born.

The Birth of the I.K.C.

Our goals:

(1) Educate

(2) Eradicate

(3) Alleviate

Education: is the key. Make people, like yourselves aware of the issues at hand and how bad it actually has become. Enlist other like-minded people to the sport aspect of legally hunting and killing iguanas. And, of course, promote iguanas as a viable renewable, sustainable food source.

Dispel the myth or misinformation about iguana hunting. Repeat after me. **Hunting iguanas is Not Illegal** in Florida or the Florida Keys.

As a matter of fact, it's promoted and encouraged because iguanas are **a non-indigenous invasive species destroying Florida's eco system**.

Iguanas currently are causing millions of dollars in property damage. You can check with the Florida Department of Agriculture and it is their stats that will tell you, "The invasions of exotic species cost Floridians over $500 million each year.

Floridians spend more than $50 million annually just to eradicate exotic weeds from our fields, pastures, canals, ponds, lakes, rivers and greens. And the economic costs are small potatoes compared to the ecological ones."

EXOTIC species by definition are not native to Florida and are introduced by human activity. They are brought in either intentionally, as ornamentals or pets, or accidentally, as hitchhikers that arrive at airports, seaports or through the mail. Florida's first European settlers brought plants and animals from their homelands including wheat, oranges, cattle and horses. Species have always moved around the globe, and the majorities are not problematic. It is today's enormous volume of global trade and travel that provides an unprecedented opportunity for species to invade. One third of all plant species in Florida are now exotic. Synonyms: <u>alien, introduced, nonnative and nonindigenous.</u>

INVASIVE exotic species are not constrained by the natural factors that existed in their native habitats–other native species, diseases and predators. Their rapid growth and spread has the potential of altering what remains of Florida's natural areas, resulting in economic or environmental harm or harm to human health and wellbeing. Fortunately, most exotic species are not invasive. **<u>Our concern is with those exotic species that have already become invasive or that are likely to become invasive in the future.</u>**
<u>Synonyms: invasive, pest or nuisance species.</u>

<u>**Eradication:**</u> Removing iguanas from this islands eco system. Prior to the start of anyone screaming or complaining about how bad or horrible it is, I'm going to tell you, this is not just my idea, it's the Florida Department of Agriculture's too. In my opinion they have a lot of clout. Here's the deal, humans caused this problem, so we have to fix it.

Alleviate: if we do our part the eco system has a chance. Become an eco-warrior, an environmentalist, it's going to help you and Florida's fragile eco system in the future.

How can you get into this?

Now I know that some of you will be saying, it's gross or disgusting or I'm a monster. And asking how could I kill and eat an iguana?

Well, honestly, it's pretty easy. Since the dawn of time if you wanted to eat, you had to hunt it, track it, catch it, massage it about the head, neck, and shoulders with a big stick or a rock and kill it. Then of course to the victor go the spoils. We call that lunch.

All living things have an aversion to dying. But that is why we are top of the line apex type predators. We as humans have been killing and eating things for thousands of years.

The good news is it's already in your DNA. From way back in the day when we were living in caves, hunting in packs, and rubbing sticks together to make fire. Remember you can't cook what you don't catch. Salad bar is for second place and as the saying goes, vegetarian is an old Indian word for bad hunter.

I'll take you back in time a little bit. The Moche people of ancient Peru worshipped animals and often depicted Green Iguanas in their art. The Green Iguana and its relative the Black Iguana *(Ctenosaura similis)* have been used as a food source in Central and South America for the past 7,000 years. It is possible that some of the populations in the Caribbean were translocated there from the mainland by various tribes as a food source. As you can tell it's nothing new. In Central and South America, Green Iguanas are still used as a source of meat and are often referred to as *gallina de palo,* (bamboo chicken or chicken of the trees) because they are said to taste like chicken. By the way the answer to that question is yes, they do taste like chicken. Iguana is a lite meat, it takes on the taste of the seasoning you apply to it.

Love the haters.

I'm going to tell you right now, if you choose this avenue there will be some people out there who are not going to agree with your decision. They will throw an ungodly temper tantrum complete with name calling, cyber bullying, and a lot of Cry baby progressive whining.

 I have found that most of those people live in their parent's basement, have a lizard on a heat rock and are residing in places that the weather would immediately kill off any invasive iguana issue.   That being said, they are not qualified to have this conversation.

Amusingly enough at the time of writing this book I posted pictures from a local hunt that was completed by myself and a couple of friends on Facebook. These pictures only showed that we removed eight large iguanas from a client's yard. These images received somewhere in the range of 173,000 views and still counting.

From that specific post on the web, I have received all manner of threats of violence including a few death threats from tree huggers, Vegans, members of PETA, and any other key board commando that you may be able think of.

The second part which in my mind was more amusing was the response I received from the local citizenry. The boots on the ground people that live here and are actually in the iguana battle daily.

The people who are cleaning up the iguana crap from their cars, boats, pools, porches, decks, docks, and paying money to fix damages caused by iguanas which have destroyed their landscaping, paint jobs and other personal property.

You name it, they are on it. I didn't have to say a word. The Locals did the bashing for me.

But I also know that perception is reality. What is perceived is believed. If you own one iguana and that is your pet. You will obviously side with your pet.

If your property is overrun with twenty, fifty, or a hundred iguanas daily, I'm pretty sure that you are going to side with me.

Here is my game plan and you are welcome to use it if you want. If you are ever attacked or harassed by some faceless keyboard commando who will no doubt call you every name in the book, and If you wish to engage in conversation with this dip dunk, and have time and inclination to attempt to defend yourself, lead them down that path.

Hand hold them a bit and explain that you are not killing iguanas for fun you are killing them as a viable food source. Add a picture of iguana tacos, or iguana soup for good measure.

This statement will make your new-found lizard loving friend's head explode.

So, after the first minor eruption continue to state that YOU are helping the environment. And are saving a fragile eco system which is in desperate need of human help.

You are honing your skill in small game hunting.

A quick note: Your target area is about the size of a dime, so get to practicing, head shots are key.

Iguanas are very hard to kill. For every iguana that is removed you have given the endangered Miami Blue Winged Butterfly a chance. Or the endangered plants that iguanas love to eat, for instance the *Cordia globosa* and the endangered Nicker Nut Tree (*Caesalpinia*) a chance

You are saving the Florida Burrowing Owl and the Gopher Tortuous (*Gopherous polyphemus*) from being evicted from their burrows by wild invasive iguanas.

Remember, just by doing what you are doing, you have not only given these plants and animals a fighting chance but you have also given 300 other species that use the unoccupied burrows that the tortuous digs in the mainland a fighting chance at survival too.

Explain that iguanas are the ENEMY of every indigenous animal in South Florida's eco system.

They are the green coated, leather jacket wearing thug on the block.

They bully their way into the burrow, eat the occupant's eggs, babies, hatchlings or whatever is inside and then take up residence as if it was meant to be.

In your closing statement advise them to look at it from a different perspective. I'm not killing iguanas. I'm saving butterflies.

Who could be mad at someone who goes out of their way to save butterflies?

Remember only you can prevent an iguana invasion.

Look what happened, we just went from being bad evil mean hunters who want to kill stuff to environmentalist. I won't tell if you don't.

Q & A

Q: Why are you killing iguanas?

A: To help save a fragile eco system. Save an island environment, limit damage caused by iguanas, promote the sport of small game hunting, and to exploit a viable sustainable food source.

Q: Is iguana hunting legal in Florida?

A: Yes. Iguanas are non-indigenous invasive species in Florida, South Florida, & the Florida Keys. Meaning they are not from here. The fine people at the Department of Agriculture will tell you that there is no iguana season, size limit or bag limit. No one is coming to arrest you for shooting iguanas. The Department of Agriculture, FWC, or any of the other law enforcement agencies actually all promote the legal hunting and eradication of iguanas.

Q: Where can I hunt iguanas?

A: Private property. If you or a friend own or have permission to use the property that has been overrun by iguanas, hunt it. Farms. Other opportunities such as but not limited to farms, ranches, gardens, fruit orchards, river banks or any place that iguanas are causing a problem and you can get permission to hunt from the land owner.

Q: Can I use a firearm, rifle, and pistol?

A: Yes. If you are on your own private property, and not located in town or a residential area close to housing. You can use firearms, small caliber rifles, pistols, bow & arrows, cross bows, sling shots. Catch them in live traps whatever you need to take care of business.

Now if you are in town or residential area, in my opinion air rifles are the way to go specifically because they are not firearms by statute. Practice firearms safety and marksmanship; head shots are the key.

Q: Can you eat iguana?

A: Yes. People have been eating iguana for 7000 years. In South America it's called chicken of the tree, in Key West it's the green tree squirrel. This book promotes the eating of iguana, check out some of the recipes. The meat is just like chicken. The tail is the white meat, the legs are the dark meat.

Q: What does iguana taste like?

A: Depends on your interpretation of food. It is a very lean meat that takes on any seasoning well. Iguanas are vegetarians, so you won't have to deal with parasites like when hunting carnivores or omnivores. My experience tells me the taste of iguana may vary from person to person. I have had people tell me it tastes like everything from chicken, pork, and even frog legs.

Q: I have this person trolling me and telling me how horrible I am because I'm hunting iguanas, they say they are going to report me to everyone. The city, county, state law enforcement agencies, the Facebook police, what do I do?

A: One of those guys. Remember an asshole is an asshole. And perception is reality. Most likely this person has a pet iguana, lives alone in the basement of his/her parents' house or are all alone in some large city. Insert city here just pick one, (New York, New

Jersey, Chicago, Colorado, Michigan, or Ohio) these are the states that seem to have the highest butt hurt rate by viewing people hunting iguanas. Amusingly enough all of the above mentioned places have something called WINTER which of course kills iguanas dead. Winter is Mother Nature's solution to the iguana problem. If you wish to engage these people in meaningful conversation, just tell them to put **RAT** in the place of the word **IGUANA** right before the word **HUNTING** and see if they feel the same way.

If that doesn't work ask them this question. Why do large cities like Chicago have The Bureau of Rodent Eradication and RAT Patrols to stop RATs from hitting epidemic levels?

How do you find iguanas to hunt?

Open your eyes. If you live in South Florida, go to your door, open it up, and take a peek outside. Odds are you will see one. Search the yards, under and around houses, tree lines, river banks, mangroves, golf courses, parks, play grounds, and swimming pools. Iguanas are smart and adaptable they can take up residence anywhere. All they need to make some place their home is have a hole in a fence, be larger or outnumber other animals that are in the general area, and all that is left is air and opportunity and they are the masters of that methodology.

If you own the property, it's a no brainer. If you don't, ask permission to hunt on other people's private property. You may be surprised how many people want these pests gone from their property. In addition, I have found that you can make a little money doing it too.

Take baby steps. Learn the craft, look for them, and before you know it you have become an iguana bounty hunter. Depending on the area, you may have to be a little more covert about your iguana hunting operations.

Tools of the trade.

So now you have decided to get down to business. You are going to need some toys from the tool box, so you can plan your backyard safari. But first a safety brief.

Remember the 4 rules of gun safety.

1. **Never point the gun at something you're not going to destroy.**
2. **Never Load the gun until you are ready to shoot.**
3. **Know your target and what's behind it. WHERE IS THAT ROUND GOING IF YOU MISS?**
4. **Never put your finger on the trigger until you are ready to shoot.**

MOST IMPORTANT RULE
(KEEP YOUR DAMN BOOGER HOOK OFF THE BANG SWITCH!)

Currently my go to pellet gun of choice is the Air Force Condor P.C.P Air Rifle. Its not a super high-end air rifle but it is very accurate and widely used in the United States for pest control small game hunting and target shooting. And a price range that wont break the bank.

It shoots a .22 caliber pellet which leaves the barrel anywhere from 900 -1400 ft. per second depending on how I have the pressure adjusted.

As far as lethality, it's just like a real .22 rifle except you won't get in trouble with the law for discharging a firearm in public.

It's great for in town, the back yard, the mangroves, a friend or clients house who needs a little help with an iguana problem or just precision plinking.

This particular air rifle is a little higher on the price range, it's approximately $800 dollars, but as you know, Mama meant business and at that time money was not an issue.

Now if finances are an issue. Or you are just starting out, I would suggest the Gamo Whisper. It comes in .177 or .22 caliber break barrel design.

Or the Benjamin Pump Action. Both of these air rifles are a little easier on the wallet. You'll want something that leaves the barrel at around 700 ft. per second. But for the most part any modern Air rifle will do the job.

I have people in the IKC who are going old school primitive style and hunting iguanas using blow guns, bow and arrows. A Cuban rig which is usually just a noose on a long cane poll.

While others, who have more property in a less urban environment are using firearms. Shot guns, .22 Magnums, and a 17 HMR for those long-distance shots on the levies up in the Everglades and the Redlands all the way to Broward and Palm beach counties on the east coast of Florida. And as you can see, they are getting some nice trophy lizards.

Promoting the proper principles and placement of precision driven projectiles.

The simple fact is, all pellets that you purchase today that are used in modern air rifles combined with the proper shot placement will kill small and even medium sized game. Here is the Geek stuff. The kinetic energy of a pellet is equal to ½ the product of the mass of that pellet and the square of the speed the pellet is moving, or for the math geek out there simply (1kg*(m/s)^2").

Pellets in laymen's terms the lighter weight or grain pellets fail to have the knock down power of the heavier grain pellets. I have shot with them all. But I have concluded that my air rifle prefers the heavier grain pellets all the way up to the 23 grain round nose slugs for when I want to make sure that a really large iguana will not just walk off after a shot.

If your pellet isn't accurate, you are wasting your time. Picking the proper ammunition or pellets for plinking, target practice, pest removal and hunting is almost as important as picking the right air rifle, and in a lot of cases the right pellet is the key to a successful hunt.

Do your homework. There are all sorts of different styles and brands of pellets to choose from. Anything from the old Daisy, Crossman, & Gamo brands just like the ones your daddy used as a child, all start out at the lower end in the price point. This is the bunch of pellets jammed in a can for a few dollars program.

All the way up to the higher priced H&N Sports or custom-made pellets which can be ordered to specific grains or weights which equates to a lot less pellets in that can for a little more money.

Air gunning is a very popular sport around the world and covers areas like basic to advanced target or bench rest shooting competitions, speed shooting, small game hunting and commercial or residential pest removal. All the aforementioned sports have a specific pellet for the specific job at hand.

Did you ever wonder what happens to those birds that get inside the grocery store and take up residence in the produce or fresh meat section and crap all over the place?

Well there's a guy for that. Hell, there are people out there taking head shots at Eurasian doves, coyotes, gophers, iguanas and golf balls at distances of 100 yards or more and surgically hitting neutralizing the target.

As stated, a friend of mine has a crew of shooters and runs guided iguana hunting safaris in Puerto Rico removing 1,600 lbs. of iguana for the farmers out there in just a few days.

Now that's what I call shooting Tex, but let's get back to reality for a minute.

In the beginning, I don't expect you or anyone else to be taking fifty or hundred-yard shots to snipe a lizard or hit any target.

First of all there are very few places in the Florida keys that have that kind of land available for an Urban hunter.

 Second, that type of skill takes years of practice to be able to achieve those types of precision shots.

But, we all have to start somewhere. So, pick up the gun, grab yourself a tin of pellets, get you a nice safe place in the back yard, basement or anywhere with a safe backdrop, and run a few hundred rounds of the regular pellets though your gun, and see how it does.

Then start experimenting go to a higher grain or weight of pellet.

Get comfortable with a little distance 10, 15, 20, or even 25 yards to start out with.

Realistically those are most likely the distance that you are going to be shooting at. Once you get dialed in and find that sweet spot, you are ready to Rock on a backyard Safari.

Shot Placement
Where do I shoot an iguana?

My philosophy is, aim little, miss little.

So, I practice putting all my shots inside a dime sized circle at a distance of usually 20-25 yards because realistically that is my cranial vault target area on an average sized iguana.

We always want to dispatch the animal in the quickest, and most humane way possible.

 As my wife has a way with words also. She says you have to be "**lethally compassionate.**"

 As a matter of fact, the number one thing that will get you in trouble when hunting, is the perception by non-hunters or anyone else that you are torturing an animal to death. And let's be honest if you are into torturing animals you're basically one step away from being a serial killer. Inhumane hunting practices will get you in both civil and criminal trouble. This is the main reason that we practice, practice, and practice some more.

Remember, perfect practice makes perfect lethal shots, and perfect shot placement is the key to a successful hunt.

I'll tell you from experience if your just starting out there is no way that you are going to shoot every iguana you target stone dead on the first shot. Take the time to get to know the tools of the trade. Some air rifles are very particular about the types of ammunition they use.

Head shots are the best if you can target that specific area (**destroy the brain and there is no pain**).

Because it's a reptile (upper torso) heart and lung shots are not as quick to kill the animal but make no mistake they are just as effective as a head or cranial vault shot. The iguana will die, but it will not be as immediate as a head shot. You will still notice some movement which will be Nerves.

If you do not make a lethal shot placement with the first shot, be ready for an immediate follow up shot with round two, to dispatch the reptile as quickly and efficiently as possible.

After your first shot, even if the head is completely gone you will most likely see the tail moving or the lizard twitching. This is the nervous system at work.

Personally, I always like to follow up with the *Cou de Gra* right to the back of the brain pan. I consider it a professional courtesy that solves the iguana twitching problem, realistically it is the most humane thing to do, and there is no further need for discussion regarding the animal suffering. Tag and bag it.

No Carcass, No credit.

Boys and girls this is a high stakes Safari here. We're eco warriors and need a body count. There are millions of iguanas out there so we can't just take your word for it. That would be too much like a fish story. As in fishing **No Carcass, No Credit!**

NOTE: All iguanas are fare game. So, don't just target the large males. Although they look more impressive they are only good for breeding. The egg bearing female counts for extra points. 40 – 70 extra points to be exact. If you see an iguana nest. Dig it up, pour cold water in it or fill it with cement or rocks. Any thing to prevent next seasons hoard from hatching.

Now that you got you a carcass, what are you going to do with it?

Congrats on your first official kill. You are now in the club. Now you can dig up a recipe for chicken of the tree or Key West green tree squirrel or the more elusive leather necked, spiny tailed grave gopher (if you fast forward you will find a few in the back of this book).

Don't worry people have been eating iguana for the last thousand years. As a matter of fact if you take a trip to South America you will find it on the menu. It's just like chicken soup.

Any recipe that you can think of that you add chicken, you can add iguana. In Honduras, El Salvador, Nicaragua, and Puerto Rico, iguana is prepared for young and old alike to give them strength and virility. A friend of mine from El Salvador called them "Mexican Viagra"

He explained that in his country iguana eggs are considered to be an aphrodisiac and a delicacy.

They are traditionally placed in soups or boiled and put on a plate with dipping sauces.

If you like egg salad you are in luck. Iguanas lay 40 to 70 eggs in a clutch.

After you shoot a pregnant female, open her up, remove the eggs, clean, wash, and boil for about 10 to 15 minutes. Presto! Egg salad in an easy convenient single serving, leather like containers. Snip the top, place between your lips, and squeeze.

Not convinced? Here is a bit of trivia. The Catholic Church has been in the game for quite a while. The church declared iguanas to be type of fish and can be eaten on meatless holidays.

Using pets to patrol the area.

So you already know that Iguanas have no natural predators in Florida, so for area denial I deploy the use of pets and their natural protective instincts and prey drive to help chase off iguanas. Take your time and teach the puppies the proper procedures for patrolling areas of operation for an iguana access denial program. Any dog will work. Pugs to Poodles, Dachshunds to Doberman, Rat Terriers to Rottweilers any old pound puppies will do.

Desperate times require desperate measures. This is war. Dogs are a great tool in this area.

If they have any sort of prey drive, meaning they will chase a ball, they will chase an iguana.

All one must do is exploit it. It's a game and dogs have been playing it for survival for thousands of years.

To enforce this action, go out with the puppy and patrol the back yard. Say, "Lizard hunt!" Point out the iguanas and let the dogs do what come natural chase, rattle, and roll.

After each successful mission praise the puppy for doing a good job.

Hell, I even have a friend who has an old alley cat that gets into hunting lizards bringing back the trophy to her owners' bed. Bringing her a little gift.

Whatever works at getting the job done, I say the more the merrier.

On a side note, DO NOT let your pet chew on or eat iguanas. First, they want to come back and give you a kiss. Second, a lot of pet owners have reported that their animals get sick and must be taken to the vet.

Err on the side of caution.

Know your foe.

The iguana is quite possibly the perfect combination of form meets functionality. It's a dinosaur from the past living in the present. A high-speed, low drag, armor plated reptile and its defensive arsenal packs a punch: claws, teeth, and a whipping long tail. If you think the teeth are a joke, pound for pound these lizards have the bite force of an alligator. Given the opportunity they will slice like a ninja and cut like a razor blade.

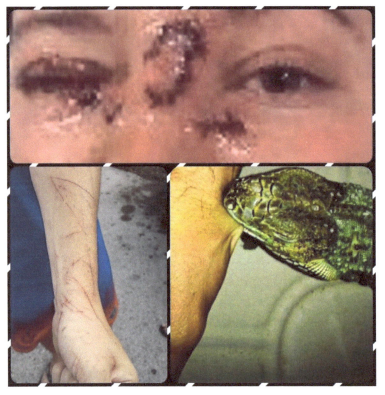

Don't believe me test the theory. Get between a big male iguana and a prospective female in mating season, more than likely he will break you off a bit of the good news and then leave you with some fine parting gifts in the form of a bight mark or two, some scratches, bleeding, and a few scars, to help you remember your experience. And for you pet owners out there, sometimes your iguana just instinctively knows it's mating season and starts wreaking havoc in the household or neighborhood.

But iguanas usually warn a person before attacking. Look for the following signs that shit is about to get real.

The dewlap.

This is that piece of skin or flap of skin under the iguana's head that just hangs there. The dewlap is used to communicate. There are several things that an iguana can say with their dewlap extended. First, an extended dewlap can simply be a greeting of hello. Or used to adjust its temperature, heat up or cool its body, but most generally it is used as a territorial display.

Secondly, it can be a form of protection. A threatened iguana extends its dewlap to make itself look larger, in hopes this action will intimidate a predator or other male iguanas into thinking the iguana is much larger than it really is.

Thirdly, an extended dewlap combined with other body language can be interpreted differently. So basically, it's important to see the big picture when reading body language.

Head bobbing.

This is one of the most noticeable forms of body language iguanas use to communicate. They cannot bark, growl, howl, or scream so we are back to body language. The way an iguana bobs its head can tell a lot about what it's trying to say. Head bobbing lets every other thing around them know they can see them, they believe they're in charge, and they are in control of this specific territory. Males usually bob more than females, especially after they have become sexually mature. The females bob their heads also, but usually not as often or as distinctively as males.

A slow, up and down bobbing of the head like a boat rolling on the ocean usually means it is just letting you know that it knows you are there and it wants you to know that it's there. This slow bobbing is normal and very common for male iguanas and should be expected. A faster motion indicates that it may be agitated and could possibly be a sign of aggression. The shudder bob is another form of head bobbing and is a rapid side to side motion. Shudder bobbing a pretty good indicator that the iguana does not want to be messed with.

Now combine all of the above, up, down, left and right, in a rapid-fire succession boys and girls this is a clear sign that the iguana is extremely irritated, and you should not be messing with it.

Tongue flicking.

As with most animals an iguana's most important sense is its sense of sight, followed closely by taste and smell. The tongue flick is used to get more information about something in the area. This behavior is a normal sight. Iguanas are reptiles and use their tongue for sensory purposes. Iguanas will often flick their tongue at food, new or strange objects (including people, animals, water or other objects), tongue flicking can be and indicator of an iguana becoming irritated, or maybe it's trying to learn a little bit more about its surrounding.

Posturing iguanas.

One very impressive form of body language is the posturing an iguana does. There is a good way an iguana postures and a very, very bad way.
Seeing a posturing iguana for the first time can almost be funny, although this amusement will be short lived when the iguana gets its way or starts to cause serious damage.
The good form can usually be seen when it's comfortable and content. A very happy iguana, lounging around, basking in the sun or being petted will stretch its front legs, standing up tall and raising its head in the air. It is said when an iguana is being petted, it will rise up, close its eyes and some will even claim that it cracks a smile.

Now, for the bad form of posturing. It involves the iguana turning its side towards you and puffing up (creating a larger profile), combined the puffing action with a slow, legs-stretched-out creeping type of walk combined with a wagging tail. This form of posturing is sometimes called **hatchet mode**. If the iguana is irritated or intimidated by you (or someone or anything else in the general vicinity).

The trifecta of fun is when the iguana combines the posturing, opens its mouth nice and wide showing you all of its small razor-sharp teeth, while slowly creeping towards your position just close enough to hit you with a nice, quick tail whip. Or if you just happen to let it get even closer you may receive a dangerous bite.

These are all indicators or a form of posturing that this is not the lizard you should be kissing up on.

These are very clear signs of aggression and should be taken *very* seriously.

 A few other examples of hatchet mode are If you notice an iguana's body all puffed up, dewlap extended and of course, the evil eye they're dishing out while gazing in your general area.

Squirming.

A squirming iguana is another obvious sign of irritation. If an iguana is squirming around in your hands, it isn't happy being held by you.

You can be bit, tail whipped and scratched.

There are two schools of thought of what you should do next when dealing with a squirming iguana.

One side may say that it is better to let the iguana go, until it decides it wants to be held.

The other options is grab that lizard and hold on tight, it's going to be a rocking, rolling reptile rodeo. Let that lizard know who's in charge.

While you may relieve some stress by letting it go when it wants to, you may be training it to do what it wants to do. Just like a bad child throwing a temper tantrum theory.

But we are not talking about training iguanas here just the body language.

Charging.

 A charging iguana is a dangerous one. If you have ever had an iguana charge you, you will know shit just got serious. The signs are obvious and usually involve a large male iguana charging in attack mode. This action is usually due to breeding season aggression, or it may be a sign that there is something physically wrong with the iguana.

Tail whipping.

You can't stop an iguana from whipping its tail at you, but you can prevent being hit by it.

This is a very obvious form of body language. Whipping its tail is usually the first *weapon* an iguana will use to protect itself. Being whipped by an iguana tail flying at near the speed of light is usually just a very painful experience, but a preventable one.

Iguanas have speed combined with very good aim and the painful experience of a good tail whip will amaze the hell out of most people whom have never experienced it.

First of all, if you are paying attention, an iguana will usually show other signs that they are irritated before cracking the whip.

Remember that whole section on posturing? Secondly, look for twitching or wagging of the tail before it attacks with it.

 If you recognize these signs, and remove yourself from the area you should be safe.

If not, you will probably just receive a nice welt as a parting gift.

The bite.

If you just got bit or you're being bitten this is an indicator that you were not paying attention, and something is going horribly wrong.

This may involve a trip to the bath room and a band aid or a trip to the Emergency room for stitches.

The bite is yet another very obvious form of body language.

An iguana may bite you for several reasons, it scared, hungry, irritated or just because it feels like it.

Usually, biting is an iguana's last form of defense.

The best possible way to prevent being bit by an iguana is to be cautious of their warning signs that have been listed on the previous pages.

The tongue flicking, posturing, slow creepy walking all the way to slowly opening its mouth prior to bite.

Most of the time iguanas will give you a very clear sign that trouble is ahead. If you got bit then you probably were not paying attention and deserved it.

The total package in the predatory concept.

Iguanas are the all-wheel drive assault vehicles of the animal world. It crawls, walks, runs, slithers, slides, digs holes, climbs trees, rocks, walls, and it swims too.

It will go over, under or around any obstacle put in its path.

That's right, no fear of the water, son. They will head to it like an Olympic swimmer.

If threatened they will run, jump, flip, flop and fly off any sea wall, dock, deck, or tree limb. Fold their legs back, hold their breath, and dive straight down to the bottom of whatever pool, creek, pond, river, ocean, or body of water they land in; iguanas whip their tails into full gear, and can hold their breath for about 30 minutes or until they make it to the other side. Whichever comes first.

Iguanas also come with a kick ass factory direct camouflage package right out of some sci-fi special ops play book. They can change color almost at will and blend into any environment the iguana may find itself in.

If the animal is cold, it collects the warmth of the sun by turning a darker color; if it's warm it deflects it away.

Most importantly they do not know the meaning of the word die.

How to eat an iguana:

The basic mechanisms of eating iguana are much the same as it was thousands of years ago. And just like anything else. One piece at a time.

1. You must locate the iguana.
2. Catch it and massage its head, neck, chest or breast area vigorously with some sort of a pellet, bullet, arrow, bladed, or blunt object until decapitation and death occurs and the life force is removed from the animal.
3. Skin, clean, cut, and carve the meat to desired size, texture or portions needed for you dish.
4. Add spices, Salt, pepper, curry, onions, and other food multipliers or ingredients such as beans & rice, potatoes, & carrots are usually the norm
5. Build a big ass white man style fire and proceed to Fry, bake, boil, or shish kabob.
6. Cook until you achieved desired smell, taste or texture.
7. Get to eating your exotic iguana dinner.

Gross! Disgusting! Eat a lizard?

What's in a Name?

You picked up this book, so that in and of itself tells me that you do not have an aversion to hunting or eating.

Ahh! We have something in common already. You have put a foot forward in the right direction. You see we are not so different after all.

Most people's problem with eating iguana is currently most of our food sources come in pretty wrapped packages, or are steaming hot from a drive through, convenience store restaurant, food cart, or other style of eatery.

We as people have no idea where it came from or what's actually in it. As long as you get a large order of fries and a cold drink you're ok.

People no longer have to catch, kill, or clean the carcass of whatever food source that has been provided by the gods to help sustain their own fragile life form. This part of daily life has been sanitized and separated from our existence.

If you are still having reservation, I can promise that it is not the worst thing you have ever eaten. Case in point, have you ever asked yourself what part of the dog does a hot dog come from? Do you know what's actually in bologna?

Ig this makes you uncomfortable, do like we humans always do when we are uncomfortable change the name. *Escargot*, is a snail. Squab is a pigeon. Iguana can be: Chicken of the Tree, Key West Tree Squirrel (*polio de guya*), Bamboo Chicken; AHH, now it sounds exotic. We are having an exotic game dinner.

Why not? At the very least you can identify what it actually is, and in this day and age of the no GMO, no antibiotics, eating free rage, organic, iguana is the perfect answer. It's non-fat lean meat. It works just as well in recipes that use chicken or fish. And seriously, we both know that you have already eaten food that you can't identify.

I can almost guarantee that. Don't believe me? It's time to test the theory. Just ask yourself what part of an animal does a hot dog come from? Not sure? That's because you have never seen a hotdog in the wild have you?

I'll help you out. It's a conglomeration of pig parts. Hot dogs are mostly made up of lips and assholes. Rooters, tooters and other pig parts that most people couldn't and wouldn't be able to identify with a sharp stick and identification chart. All thrown into a giant bucket, dumped into a grinder and ground up. Then conveniently packed into a sausage skin, slapped in a pretty package, shipped to your local supermarket where you purchased it. Slapped a little fire to it, add a bun, some condiments mayo, mustard, ketchup and PRESTO! You just ate an asshole sandwich and liked it!
Now remember. No matter what kind of spices you use, an asshole is still an asshole.

A few other things you may have paid ungodly prices for someone to put on your dinner plate and were ok with it just due to the name change or it being socially acceptable. For instance, *escargot* is just a fancy word for snail or slug. You want to make pigeon extra pricy? Call it squab. The reality is, it's just a flying rat with wings. Lobster is nothing more than a salt water cockroach. Crawfish, a miniature lobster caught in a swamp is a freshwater cockroach. Alligator, talk about an ugly animal, a lot bigger than an iguana, but taste just as good and has more meat to it.

If you're still offended by iguana, could you venture a guess as to what Rocky Mountain Oysters may possibly be? I'll give you a hint. It has nothing to do with sea food. If you have not guessed yet, the answer is calf balls.
You see we Americans already eat weird food. The problem is you can't identify the entire aforementioned item prior to recognizing a hot dog in its natural form. Yes sir, just think, you're turning your nose up at iguana stew, BBQ iguana, or meat on a stick. But you'll eat a hot dog?

So, let me be the first to welcome you to the Key West version of P.E.T.A. Not the normal one that may be running through your head but the island equivalent, People Eating Tasty Animals.

Baby steps.

If you're not into eating, just hunting. Well, it is buzzard bait and they need to eat too. Or the fisherman love putting then into crab traps, apparently, they make great bait.

 Note to self, if you are hunting on somebody else's property's it is highly frowned upon to just leave dead lizard laying around the yard to stink up the place. Please pick up your iguana on the way out and place it in a grave, trash can, or a dumpster somewhere.

Field cleaning your lizard.

Bush meat vs traditional skinning. As the saying goes, there's several ways to skin a cat, or in this case an iguana. If you have never hunted or cleaned wild game and need a good visual check out my YouTube channel: **Iguana Killers Club: Field Dressing an Iguana**; I'll show you how to do it step by step.

Now if you're down in the islands of Trinidad, Tobago, or any other place in South America the ritual is most likely the same. Once they get it, as they say, it's on like Donkey Kong! Someone immediately starts a small fire which is used to singe the parasites, skin and scales which are then scraped off with a knife as the iguana is continuously slowly rotated over the smoking flaming brush fire.

Next it is gutted cleaned and divided into pieces, and either placed directly onto the fire for original recipe, or extra crispy; baked iguana taste like chicken with the slight smoky after taste.

Put it into a cooking pot with a little oil, add some vegetables, a few peppers, an onion, curry and other various seasoning stir vigorously, add some rice and before you know it dinner is served.

This technique also works if you scald the iguana in a pot of boiling water. It's just like old school back on the farm chicken preparation. Of course, that would be prior to the Colonel, Popeye's, or Churches breaking bad on the new and improved fried chicken assembly line.

The original porch to pan action. One minute free range yard bird, walking around aimlessly, scratching dirt, chasing bugs, and cackling at whatever came along. The next it was snagged, head removed from its normal resting location on its neck, then plunged into a bucket of boiling water, plucked cleaned of all offending feathers, and anointed with fire to singe the hangers on. It was then cut, drawn, quartered, dipped, battered, and dunked into a deep fryer. Ten minutes later someone's mother would be adding mashed potatoes and corn on the cob three ways: quick, fast and in a hurry.

Now back to the iguana.

The goal is to scald the skin and remove all the scales, dirt, or parasites and to prepare it for meal time.

The way I do it may be a little different, but the outcome is the same. After I kill it I put it on ice to stiffen it up bit. I take a good sharp knife, make an incision at the anus and cut it from the tooter to the rooter, making sure I do not puncture the intestines. Remove all the entrails from the body cavity. Save the heart and liver for soup, or the frying pan (they come up extra crispy).

Next step is to chop off the head and all four claws. Everything else is going to the trashcan or crab trap. Remember Iguana parts make great bate for lobster pots or crab traps

After that, I make another incision straight down the legs and tail. Once those cuts are made, work your fingers between the meat and skin. Give it a tug or three and eventually it will come off like a rented tuxedo.

What you have in front of you is what is getting rinsed, cleaned, divided into bite sized portions, seasoned, and cooked up.

The meat should be light pink, and once it is skinned and cleaned it shouldn't have a strong smell.

What does iguana taste like?

Would you be mad if I told you it tastes like chicken? Because it tastes like chicken.

There are a lot of variables. Depending on what the iguana's diet consisted of is what you will experience. For instance, if the iguana was living in a mango tree or papaya tree, the meat will most likely take on a sweet taste.

Now if it was up in a mangrove bush munching on leaves it goes back to regular iguana. It also depends on what you season it with, but normally most of the people who I have fed iguana to (including myself) have said it was a cross between chicken, pork or frog legs.

Depending on how it's prepared, the meat can be a little stringy. The biggest portion of meat comes from the legs and the tail. And watch out for the bones.

Since iguanas are vegetarians you won't have a lot of parasites to deal with as with carnivores.

My first iguana experience.

It was sometime back in 2013, I was doing what I normally do when I started to notice the green horde arrive in droves. If I had the time, inclination & opportunity to thin the herd a bit, that's what I did.

Now at this point, I was not actively hunting iguanas. I was targeting the ones that got into my back yard, which of course, as you know from your previous reading, is classified as an iguana no-go zone.

This is where they get selectively targeted, shot, and removed from the area with a professional vengeance.

On this specific day my neighbors, who at the time were a group of roofers from various parts of South America including El Salvador, Guatemala, Honduras, and Nicaragua. They had just rented and moved into the house next door.

They just so happened to be collectively meandering in their back yard and were having some kind of group after work party /fiesta/ siesta event, slamming a few cold beers, blasting Mariachi music with a few cut-ins of what sounded like Spanish rap, and discussing roofer shit in their native tongues. All of this while attempting to hand line snapper from the dock.

They noticed me shoot out into the mangroves and knock a rather large lizard from a tree branch about 30 yards away.

At this point the music came to an abrupt *el halto*! The lead guy walked to the fence line and asked, "Did you just choot that iguana?"

I replied, "If you're referring to the one that just fell out of the tree and into the water the answer is yes."

He then asked, "What you gonna do with it?"

My response was, "Not sure. Why you want it?"

Nodding his head in the north and south positions, he asked, "How much?" Then proceeded to hold up four ice cold beers from the Budweiser category.

"SOLD!" I said, and started snatching the beers out of his little calloused hand before he could change his mind.

That man jumped out of his boots, threw his keys and cell phone on the deck, and made it into the canal before I could pop the top off of the first of my newly acquired frosty beverages.

Upon completion of his pants off dance off, I decided to put the pellet rifle down, sit back, and watch the show unfold and enjoy more of my cold beer.

Like an Olympic swimmer he retrieved the floating soggy iguana, then swam back and crawled up onto his deck, and started butchering it right there.

The music was once again activated and set the tempo as the pocket knife was sterilized with a shot of tequila and then rinsed down with half of an already open beer.

The group of men gathered to apparently provide managerial support in the field dressing of the four foot iguana carcass which was now taking up residence in their backyard.

When he opened it up he found out that it was a pregnant female which just happened to be slap full to the gills with little iguana eggs.

 Ladies and gentlemen, it would seem this meant something to these fine gentlemen. Because that is when the real whooping and hollering began.

It was at this point in the iguana cesarean section the guy jumps up and comes over holding a hand full of eggs and asks, "Hey man, you ever have iguana eggs?"

"No" I replied and shook my head in the normal east & west position.

He then said, "You give me 15 minutes and I'm gonna make you something good." He disappeared in midst of drunken Mexicana music festival, cigarette smoke and the rest of the group pounding the *cervesa's*.

As promised he returned as I was in the middle of beer number three, feeling slightly amused at the fan fair while contemplating a business plan involving future iguana assassination and trading them to people from South America for cold beer.

Due to my current situation it would seem there is a market for wholesale iguana and apparently if they have eggs, that sir, looks like an added bonus.

I'm about to turn into Colonial friggin' Sanders with the deep fried Chicken of the tree here.

So, my new found friend arrived bearing gifts of boiled iguana eggs in a red plastic bowel.

He presented me with a fork and some fresh homemade picante sauce. Then began to explain how this was a delicacy back home; iguana eggs are packed full of vitamins minerals, and if you eat the eggs you will be chasing the old lady around the house because iguana eggs are Mexican Viagra.

I laughed a little bit and cracked the last beer figuring what the hell, vitamins, minerals, and chasing the old lady around the house, nothing wrong with that.

Iguana eggs are in a leathery pouch, so you have to cut, snip, bite or tear the top portion open to get to the actual egg yolk on the inside.

 My new friend advised me to put a little sauce in the egg prior to eating. The sauce consisted of salt, pepper, ground up hot peppers, and a little garlic mixed in with a little vinegar. It wasn't your mama's hot sauce, but worked like a champ.

So, I cut a slice in the top of the egg, slipped the lizard egg between my teeth, applied a little bit of pressure and pulled.

The contents squeezed into my mouth and ill be damned if it didn't taste just like egg salad.

And that is actually the best description that I can give you, is egg salad.

If you like egg salad that is exactly what you are getting. Egg salad in single bite size serving; add hot sauce to taste and you are golden. Put it on a cracker, bread or direct deposit it in your mouth.

Just think, vitamins, minerals, and Mexican Viagra in one pouch. All that from a backyard safari.

Now were going to get to the good stuff. I have a couple of recipes for you to try.

Only for the most daring or the hungriest in the bunch. Dock to dish, porch to pan, palm tree to plate, add beans and rice, and don't be late.

In the beginning, my deal with the chefs was, my band of merry misfits will do the hunting, catching, tagging and bagging, skinning cleaning and chilling. We bring it to you and you start with the grilling.

I have scoured the lower Keys and found several chef's that have taken up the challenge of iguana cooking.

Some are old world recipes. Like the fine people at Jose's II who graced my plate with Nicaraguan style Iguana BBQ, Iguana Peace Stew, and a dish called Iguana Pinole.

I dropped off a bag of lizard meat and let Jose' do the rest. I came back a few hours later to strap on the feed bag.

Just for fun I brought along a group of friends of mine who just happened to be visiting from Missouri. We videotaped the event for good measure. Low and behold everyone had a great meal and no one left the table hungry.

At a separate event the fine people at Blossoms Cajun Kitchen, Chef Jose' and Tommy concocted two separate dishes using the rowdy reptiles for a little garden party get together.

First being Sweet Teriyaki Brazed Iguana. The meat came from the tail which is predominantly white meat. Marinated in sweet teriyaki sauce, it sat on a hot top and under a lid.

Next was Cajun Iguana Legs, yum. Again you cant go wrong with this stuff. From survival food to four star dining with friends and family. Get out and live a little.

Boiled Iguana Eggs

We will start this party with something simple. Boiled Eggs. Who can't boil an egg?

Ingredients:

Iguana eggs. Now don't go out and dig up an iguana den to find the eggs, make sure you get them from the source directly during field dressing.

Iguanas are known to have 20-70 eggs, so don't worry there will be enough for everybody.

Pot, add water and salt.

Bring to a rolling boil, add raw eggs and boil about 15 minutes.

Pull out, snip the tops, squeeze out the yolk, and WALAA, you have egg salad. Add hot sauce, diced pickles and you have spicy egg salad. Great for party snacks, on crackers or toast.

BBQ Iguana

All right we have been grilling food for thousands of years. If we could catch it, kill it and throw it on a fire, well that is BBQ. Chicken, steak, rabbit, fish and lobster. Lizard is no different. We have advanced our technique a bit. We have moved up to fancy out door ovens.

So first go out and get you a couple of iguanas look for a nice three foot lizards for grilling ops.

(Traditionally the people who cook iguana do not like to use the large ones. Too tuff they say).

Kill, clean, and start to cook. After cleaning up Iggy, put them in a salty brine solution and soak em. That removes some of the gamey taste and removed any excess blood. Drain off the water and pat dry

Add your seasoning salt & pepper.

Melt a little butter with vinegar, lemon or lime (if you're in the Keys), beer and baste occasionally. Put them to the fire. 15 minutes should get you started and 20 should get you done. Turn while cooking. Then if you want add BBQ sauce.

Iguana Soup

Another easy quick fix.

Catch, kill, and clean you a nice medium sized iguana. Cut it up into nice bite size portions.

A soup pot full of water salt and pepper, and spicy pepper to taste.

Add chopped veggies: carrots, celery, corn, potatoes, parsley, tomatoes, and an onion for good measure.

Put on the stove bring to a rolling boil and then dial it back a little. Let it do all the work for you. Stir occasionally until it starts smelling like mama's chicken soup. Then you are ready for a little Chicken of the Tree Soup, dig in.

Iguana Stew

Catch, kill, and clean a nice medium sized iguana. Cut it up into nice bite size portions.

Soup pot full of water salt & pepper, and spicy pepper to taste.

Add chopped veggies. Carrots, celery, corn, potatoes, parsley, tomatoes & an onion for good measure. Oh don't forget the V8. That's the secret.

Put on the stove bring to a rolling boil and then dial it back a little. Let it do all the work for you. Stir occasionally until it starts smelling like what mama used to make.

If your mama ever made iguana.

When you are ready, dig in. It's the soup that eats like a meal!

Iguana Pinole
This is another fine dish from Jose's II

Catch, kill, and clean two nice medium sized iguanas. Cut it up into nice bite size portions remove the bones. Hand them to Jose' and he will do the rest.

Two iguanas

5 cups of hominy

Spices: salt, pepper, onion, bay leaves, garlic Mexican oregano

Simmer the corn, bay leaf, garlic, and onion for about 10 minutes. Add the meat that was cleaned from the iguana and simmer for another 15 minutes.

Sweet Teriyaki Iguana

By Chef Jose' & Tommy at Blossom's Cajun Kitchen

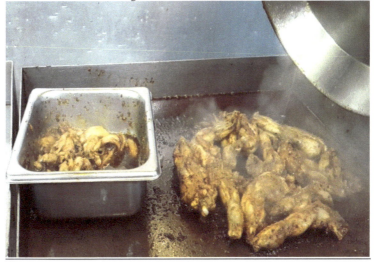

½ cup of soy sauce

4 green onion stalls chopped

½ onion chopped

5 tbsps. brown sugar

Place all ingredients into food processor or blender and blend like hell. Then pour into a sauce pan bring to a boil for about 15 minutes or until reduced by 50%. Let it cool. Place 10-20 iguana legs into the bowl and pour teriyaki sauce over the iguana legs, coating the hell out of them. Refrigerate for 30 minutes to 24 hrs. Place iguana legs into a large hot skillet on medium heat keep them moving until you think they are done the temp is approx. 160 degrees.

Cajun Style Iguana Legs or Dragon Wings

½ tsp of cayenne pepper

¼ tsp of black pepper

¼ tsp garlic powder

¼ tsp onion powder

1 tbsp. paprika

1 ½ tbsps. Kosher Salt

¼ tsp thyme

5 tbsps. olive oil.

Blend the dry spices with the olive oil and make sure it's blended well.

Cover 10-20 legs with the sauce refrigerate 30 minutes to 24 hrs. The longer the better. It lets the seasoning soak in.

Place the legs in a hot skillet, stir and keep them moving so they do not scorch. Cook until ready or internal temp reaches 160 degrees. Eat on!

Mojo Marinated Iguana

If you're in the Keys you have to know what Mojo is. The best marinade for chicken, pork, fish and now iguana too.

Catch, kill, and clean you a nice medium sized iguana or two. Cut it up into nice bite size portions. Front quarters, hind quarters and tail have the most meat on it. The ribs and back are just too bony to mess with. Add more iguanas to the pot. Don't worry we won't run out of them anytime soon.

(1) Place in a zip lock of Mojo for a couple of hours or overnight.

(2) When ready to cook, warm that oven up to 375 degrees.

(3) Place in a cooking pan, cover and roast 20 minutes or until tender.

(4) Serve with beans & rice.

If you want to get fancy slap some mixed veggies on the side.

Iguana Taco

To make you a bunch of Dragon Taco's get ready to add the hot sauce, guacamole, and some corn tortillas. Presto! We got taco sling.

>1 iguana
>
>1 large onion
>
>1 large avocado
>
>1 radishes
>
>2 garlic cloves
>
>1 bunch of cilantro
>
>Corn tortillas

Cook in salt water until the meat is tender then remove from the bones.

While your lizard is cooking, chop the radishes and cilantro for garnish on the tacos.

Use the other half of the onion and avocado make guacamole.

Add ½ of the chopped onion, garlic, and iguana meat to the hot pan, fry with a tablespoon of oil on medium until it gets brown. Add meat to a tortilla pieces of onion, radish, and avocado then add hot sauce to your liking.

Warm the tortillas in the pan, add to the plate fill with iguana meat onion garlic mixture. Top it off with cilantro and radishes. Hot sauce to taste, BOOM!!! Dragon Taco's! Rinse down with the cold beer of your choice. Don't forget the salt and lime.

Trinidad Style Curry Iguana Stew

2lbs of iguana meat
1 1/2 cups coconut milk
2 tbsps. curry
1/4 lb green papaya, peeled and chopped
½ chopped onion
3 tbsp. sugar
20 leaves chadon beni, or finely chopped cilantro
2 cloves garlic, crushed
3 tbsps. oil
seasoning to taste
salt to taste
pepper to taste

When I got this recipe I was talking to an old Trini woman who lives here in the Keys. She told me that the size of the iguana was key ingredient. Sometimes the big ones are a little tough we have to soften it in some way, and traditionally the best thing to use is green papaya. The green papaya tenderizes the meat. Or you can use nutmeg. Apparently, that's how meat was softened in Trinidad when she lived there.

Curry stewing is self-explanatory, it's just like making any other stew but you are adding curry to it. First the meat is seasoned with all your green seasonings with the curry added. Then it is left to marinate overnight. When it is time to cook the meat it is then stewed like everyone else does; with the brown sugar.

Sauté the garlic in oil and remove it put it on the side you're going to be adding it back later.

Add the sugar and allow it to caramelize to a nice reddish brown color.

Add the seasoned iguana meat and start stirring, cover everything with the brown juice and allow to simmer for about five minutes.

Then add the papaya, garlic and a little bit of water just to make it all mix together. Let simmer for about 15- 20 minutes.

Now add the coconut milk and allow to simmer until tender. Place on a bed of rice and you're eating like a champ island style.

The World Famous Green Iguana Margarita

While dinner is cooking make yourself a couple of Iguana drinks just to match the dinner event. When in Margaritaville, drink like you're in Margaretville.

    1 oz. Midori Melon Liqueur

    2 oz. tequila break out the good stuff don't skimp

    4 oz. sweet and sour mix

Or

Sleeping Lizard Margarita

This is for those who want to party like a rock star, or vomit like a hobo, and nurse a hangover like a champ the next morning.

Made just like the Green Iguana above, just double the dosage and if you are on the island add some fresh key lime juice for taste.

Blend it shake it up and pour it into a big ass margarita glass, salt the rim, add some ice, put a large straw in it, and share with a friend.

Iguana Sunrise

For those long nights when you know you're going to want to watch the sun come up, but in all seriousness, that shits not going to happen.

    1 oz. tequila

    Splash of soda

    ¾ oz. triple sec

    ½ oz. vodka

    1 ¾ oz. orange juice

    1 ¾ oz. sweet and sour mix

Slam it in the blender, push the go button, and serve in a big glass over ice garnish with an orange slice and a cherry on top.

Naked iguana

Equal parts of:

    Midori

    OJ

    Grenadine

It's kind of like trash can punch. It will get the job done. And naked is only part of it.

Pink Iguana

    1 oz. vodka

    1 oz. Amaretto

    Pink lemonade

Well it looks to be that time again. If you have made it this far and if I didn't change your mind about the iguana issue in South Florida and the Keys, hopefully I may have enlightened you a bit about the world of air rifles and the sport of small game hunting and eating exotic game.

If you think you are ready for that back yard safari, go for it.

First and foremost be safe and happy hunting. Find you a nice piece of private property, target, bag, tag and butcher you up a whole bunch of bush meat.

Fire up the stove, crockpot, kettle or back yard BBQ pit. Get to the chilling & grilling part of life.

Remember while you're hunting the number 1 rule is no one gets hurt. The rest is common sense.

Don't point a gun at anything you don't intend to destroy.

Know what your target is, what's behind It.

Most importantly, know where the round, bullet, or pellet will stop.

Don't load the gun until necessary. Keep the gun on safe, and your booger hook off the bang switch.

For Christ sake get out there, go hunting, eat something different, and have some fun.

If you liked this book there is a couple more you may be interested in. Check out Letters from the Sandbox & Corset Chronicles: Tails from a Key West Strip Club.

Thousands sold, and people still keep wanting more. So, I would say it's a good read.

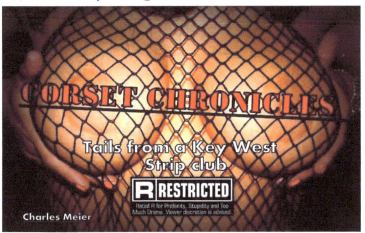

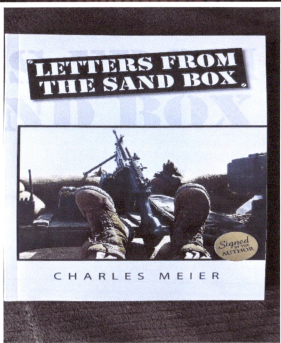

A special thanks to my buddy Jim Walton at Farm Snipers. A true brother from

Another mother. When it comes to hunting invasive species worldwide, Jim is the go to guy. He and his team travel all over the planet from Puerto Rico, Texas, Arizona Hawaii helping people solve their pest problems and restoring balance to natural eco systems. Thanks for providing that helping hand on so many different levels, not only this project and the cover art, but all the others that I have requested your assistance in also. Thanks brother.

Printed in the USA
CPSIA information can be obtained
at www.ICGtesting.com
LVHW072003110224
771576LV00001B/2